Sacred Rituals
for Every Day

ANSELM GRÜN
TRANSLATED BY NANCY DE FLON

Paulist Press
New York / Mahwah, NJ

Cover image by Imageman/Shutterstock.com
Cover and book design by Lynn Else

First published in German as *Kleine Rituale für den Alltag* copyright © 2012 Vier–Türme GmbH, Verlag, 97359 Münsterschwarzach Abtei.

English translation copyright © 2017 by Paulist Press, Inc.

Library of Congress Cataloging-in-Publication Data
    Names: Grün, Anselm, author.
    Title: Sacred rituals for every day / Anselm Grün ; translated by Nancy de Flon.
    Other titles: Kleine Rituale für den Alltag. English
    Description: New York : Paulist Press, 2017.
    Identifiers: LCCN 2016049637 (print) | LCCN 2017015707 (ebook) | ISBN 9781587686795 (e-book) | ISBN 9780809153305 (pbk. : alk. paper)
    Subjects: LCSH: Catholic Church—Customs and practices. | Days—Miscellanea.
    Classification: LCC BX2170.C56 (ebook) | LCC BX2170.C56 G7813 2017 (print) | DDC 248.4/6—dc23
    LC record available at https://lccn.loc.gov/2016049637

ISBN 978-0-8091-5330-5 (paperback)
ISBN 978-1-58768-679-5 (e-book)

Published by Paulist Press
997 Macarthur Boulevard
Mahwah, New Jersey 07430
www.paulistpress.com

Printed and bound in the
United States of America

CONTENTS

PREFACE

THE NEED FOR RITUALS TODAY IS GREAT. I HAVE ALREADY offered my thoughts about rituals and described actual rituals in different books. In this book, I would like to connect the rituals with the seven days of the week.

In the spiritual tradition, each day of the week has a special character, determined by the seven days on which God created the world. God created a particular work on each of the seven days of the week of Creation. Using these creation days as a base, we too can let each day of our week have its own prominent theme.

The Christian tradition has associated the days of the week with the redemption through Jesus Christ. From this perspective, the last three days and the first day of the week are especially noteworthy. Thursday is the day of the institution of the Eucharist, and on Friday, we reflect on the death of Jesus. Saturday is the day on which Jesus lay in the tomb, and Sunday is the day of resurrection. But even the other days have specific themes in the Church tradition. On Monday, the Church reflects on the Holy Trinity; on Tuesday, it calls to mind the angels; and on Wednesday, St. Joseph, patron saint of work. Saturday is not only the day of resting in the tomb but is also, in a special way, dedicated to Mary.

Thus, each day has its own quality. And in this book, I would like to make it possible for each of these special qualities to be experienced in everyday life through rituals.

I have chosen rituals for two weeks, and invite you, dear reader, to practice these for one week at a time. You can also alternate the rituals. If you wish, however, you can also limit yourself to the seven that appeal to you the most, and practice them each week.

The rituals will help us to experience each day with its own special quality, and to begin it in such a way that it is a blessed day and we are embraced by God's blessing. The book begins and concludes with a morning and an evening ritual, respectively, that you can use each day.

MORNING RITUAL

THE SIGN OF THE CROSS

BEGIN THE MORNING WITH A BIG SIGN OF THE CROSS. Sit or stand in an upright position and, fully conscious and aware of what you are doing, touch your forehead with your right hand. Let God's love flow into your thoughts today.

Then bring your hand down and place it on your lower abdomen. Let God's love flood your strength, your vitality, your sexuality. In so doing, imagine that God strengthens and purifies your energy so that it can be permeated by God's Spirit.

Next, place your hand on your left shoulder. Let God's love flow into your unconscious, into the images that lie dormant deep within you. Imagine that God's love brings order into all the inner chaos of your soul, lights up the darkness, and heals the images that make you ill. You can also imagine that God's love is streaming into your feminine side. Each of us has a feminine, tender, receptive side.

The feminine can bestow security—but it can also hold us back. It brings growth to one's life, and is a strong, nascent power, but it can also be smothering. When the feminine side of us is penetrated by God's love, then it becomes a blessing—for humanity and for yourself. Let God's love also flood your heart so that it is warmed by the glow of divine love.

Then place your hand on your right shoulder. Let God's love flow into your conscious: into your actions, your energy, and your decisions. Your right side is the masculine side. It can make fertile, but it can also tyrannize. It can decide, but it can also rule over everything. When God's love flows into your masculine side, it becomes a force that sets something good in motion, that supports and encourages, and that gives shape and form to something.

In the Sign of the Cross, God's love touches you so that you can feel totally accepted by and imbued with God's love. But with the Sign of the Cross you also say yes to yourself. You totally accept yourself, because everything in you is accepted, touched, and flowed through by God's love.

You can make the Sign of the Cross silently; or you can combine it with the words that are customary in our Western tradition: "In the name of the Father, and of the Son, and of the Holy Spirit." Then you sense that the triune God is penetrating everything in you.

You can also combine the Sign of the Cross with the formula that comes from the Syrian Church: "In the name of the Father, who has conceived of and formed me. And of the Son, who has descended into the depths of my humanity. And of the Holy Spirit, who turns left to right."

In the Syrian formula, what we imply with our brief Western

formula becomes clear: the Father puts the stamp on our thinking. He has created us so that we will create, form, and mold something in his name in this world. He helps us to shape this world in his Spirit. The Son has descended into our humanity. He has taken on a fleshly existence. He accompanies us. He descends with us into the depths of our unconscious in order to fill and heal everything in us with his love. The Holy Spirit is Transformer and Reconciler. He transforms the dark into light, the unconscious into the conscious, the aggressive into love, and chaos into order. And he reconciles the different areas in us that we ourselves cannot bring together. He unites that which tears each of us apart. He connects us with everything that is in us. Thus, he makes each of us one and whole.

Let God's blessing flow into the rooms of your home. Go through the rooms one by one: your bedroom, your living room, the kitchen, the workroom, and the children's room. God's blessing drives away all demons and all the strife that has sometimes nested in these places. God's blessing fills the rooms with love, with warmth, and with a good atmosphere.

Then proceed into your day with God's blessing. Let it flow to the people with whom and for whom you will be working: to your colleagues, to the customers who come to you, even to the difficult customers whom you would prefer to run away from. Envelop these people with God's blessing, too. Then, today, you will encounter them in a different way.

You can let the blessing flow into the spaces in which you work: into the factory, into the company, into the office, into the retail space. You will then have, for the entire day, the feeling that you are not going out into the cold, strange world. Instead, you are moving in blessed spaces in which the people who work or shop are also blessed.

In the Gospel of Luke (6:28), Jesus invites us to bless the people who persecute us, or—another way of putting it—who curse us and speak ill of us. Many think that this is expecting too much. But try it just for once. Consider with whom you are currently experiencing difficulties and would prefer to avoid. Then let the blessing flow to this person.

When you bless the other person, you are not stuck in the victim position. You do not remain passive, but actively react. You send God's blessing and thus positive energy to this person. That does you good as well. Perhaps you will then feel freer and also protected by God's blessing. You are no longer the victim injured by the other person. You don't need to be afraid of the other's snide remarks or cursing, insulting words. You counter them with God's positive energy, which is stronger than the negative energy of aggression.

When you bless this person, you can meet him or her with greater impartiality. Instead of the other being your enemy, you see the person as blessed, and you are confident that the blessing transforms and frees the person from hardness and coldness, allowing you to meet him or her more easily.

Place yourself in an upright position and raise your hands in blessing. Point the palms of your hands forward. Then imagine God's blessing flowing through your hands to the persons with whom you feel especially connected: your spouse, your children, your parents, your relatives, and your friends. Imagine God's blessing flowing to these persons and embracing them with God's love like a cloak that keeps them warm. It protects them from all the cold that meets them from the outside.

With the Sign of the Cross and with the blessing that you send out into the world, you will have a good start to your day. Thus this day will be a blessed day, a pleasant day. You are then confident that all that you take into your hands brings a blessing, and you will meet the blessed persons in such a way that you receive a blessing from them, too.

SEVEN RITUALS
for the
FIRST WEEK

MONDAY

Light a Candle

O N MONDAY, BEGIN YOUR DAY BY LIGHTING A CANDLE. Be aware of what you are doing when you light it, and then observe the candle and the warm light that emanates from it. Imagine that this light is driving all darkness out of you. The warmth from the candle will banish all coldness from your heart. The candle will also carry this warmth into the world that greets you once again at work on Monday.

When you light the candle, you may wish to recite words from the Bible. For example, from the Prophet Isaiah: "Arise, shine; for your light has come, and the glory of the LORD has risen upon you" (Isa 60:1). In this way, the burning candle is not only a simple light but the glory of the Lord himself shining on you through this light.

Or you can recite aloud the Christmas text from Isaiah: "The people who walked in darkness / have seen a great light; / those who lived in a land of deep darkness— / on them light has shined" (Isa 9:2).

By speaking this word aloud into the candle, you feel all the darkness disappearing from your heart. And even the world, with its darkness that you meet in the daily news, is transformed and becomes full of hope.

Or say aloud to yourself the words of Jesus: "I am the light of the world. Whoever follows me will never walk in darkness but will have the light of life" (John 8:12). Thus, in the candle you experience Jesus himself, who is now present in this room and wants to fill your heart with his light.

Consider the mystery of the light. The light originates from the candle through the burning of the wax. This represents a love that consumes itself. The candle can consume itself because there is enough wax present. It does not need to save wax. But sometimes one must trim the wick; otherwise the flame becomes too high and fills the room with smoke.

There is also a love that is too raucous and wears a person out. This love does no good either to you or to the other person. The other person feels the "smoke from the candle" in the love: the ulterior motives, the things that are wished for or overdone that do not light up the other person but, rather, fill them with smoke.

The candle consists of two elements. One is the *flame*, which symbolizes the spiritual, since it rises up to heaven. (It is said of monks that their fingers become fire when they pray.) Thus, the burning candle is a symbol of our praying. A favorite custom at pilgrimage sites is to light candles and place them on an altar or before a statue of Mary. For the person who lights the candle, this is their way of saying that the prayer keeps going as long as the candle burns. And they hope that their prayer brings light into their own life, as well as into the hearts of those persons for whom they are lighting this candle.

The candle's other element is the *wax* that is consumed. For this reason, the candle in the early Church was a symbol for Christ, who is both God and human. The wax symbolizes his human nature, which was consumed for us, as he gave himself up out of love for us. The candle's flame stands for Christ's divinity.

If you look at the candle in this way—with the eyes of tradition, with the eyes of the many people who have gone before you for whom the candle was a mystery—then something quite essential about yourself and about Jesus Christ will dawn on you.

The candle points to the mystery of the incarnation. God's light shines in Jesus, who has become human. But the candle is also a symbol for our humanity.

God's light will shine in our bodies, too. We are like the burning thorn bush. We are worthless, overlooked, and dried out. And yet, at the same time, God's glory shines in us. We burn without burning up. This is the mystery of the thorn bush.

The candle says one more thing: we burn for others as well. We burn when we devote ourselves to others. We are used up just as the candle wax is used up by giving us its light and warmth. Our devotion always has two aspects. We give what we receive. We allow what bubbles up in us from the source of divine love to flow further. In this sense, we are always able to give without becoming weaker, because the source, being divine, is inexhaustible.

But then there is the second aspect as well. We consume ourselves, just as the candle wax consumes itself. If we treat the candle carefully, it burns for a longer time. But in any case, the candle will burn out. Sometimes we tell a person who overexerts oneself not to burn the candle at both ends; otherwise the candle will burn too quickly. Our strength is limited. We are not God, who can create out of infinity and out of his fullness. We are human beings. Through us and in us, God's light can shine for our fellow humans. But this also causes our wax to burn. Our candle slowly diminishes. And in one way or another, the candle will go out, thereby reminding us of our finitude and of our death. But in death, our life shines out in a new way. We become, in Christ, a light for others forever.

TUESDAY

WRITE DOWN A SAYING

O N TUESDAY, WRITE DOWN A SAYING. SAYINGS ARE made for speaking and for writing. It is in the speaking and the writing that the mystery of the saying emerges.

Recite out loud the opening words of the Gospel of John to yourself. Listen to the words that you speak. Fill the words with the sound of your voice. They burst forth from your heart and produce a mood in you. They want your heart to agree with your voice and with the words that become audible through your voice.

In the beginning was the Word, and the Word was with God, and the Word was God. He was in the beginning with God. All things came into being through him, and without him not one thing came into being. What has come into being in him was life, and the life was the light of all people. (John 1:1–4)

Listen to these words; but then also try to understand them.

You sense the energy that is hidden in the words. God has created the world through his Word. But we, too, produce a reality with our words. The Church fathers say that we build a house with words. But the question is, which house do we build with our words: a cold house, in which no one feels at home, or a house full of love and warmth; a house in which people are happy, in which they understand who they are; a house in which the words coax to the surface the life that is, too often, hidden in them?

The secret of God himself meets us in these words. In each word that we speak, something of the Word that is with God and that is God himself resonates.

With our words we create a reality. We sense, on the one hand, how negative words that are spread by the media create an atmosphere of hate and discord, of power and destruction. Good words, on the other hand, unite people. They encourage, raise up, and give hope.

By reciting the words of the Prologue to John's Gospel aloud, you sense something of the mystery of each word. For John, the culmination of this mystery is the fact that life and light are both in the Word. Words illuminate our own existence. They bring light into the darkness. They clarify something. And words have life. We sense that words often do us good. They make us alive. They bring us into contact with the life that is at the ground of our soul but that is often submerged in everyday existence. Words awaken the life inside us once again, enticing it to come out.

Words are also meant to be written. The three great Abrahamic religions—Judaism, Christianity, and Islam—are also religions of the book. They recognize sacred scriptures. God's Word is written down. And the sacred scriptures are revered, written down over and over, and often given artistic form.

Try practicing the following ritual: Take a passage from the Bible and write it down slowly. While you write down the passage of Scripture, you may sense that you are unable to believe what you are writing. The words sound beautiful, but you actually have no idea what they mean.

You then have two possible ways of treating this passage. Either you spend twenty minutes writing this passage over and over again until it is spoken in your heart and you are able to believe it—or you simply rewrite the passage. Play and wrestle with the words, and write down what comes from your heart. Your chosen Scripture passage is like a needle that pricks your heart. And all at once everything that is in your heart comes out; all your feelings and thoughts—even those that confuse you. By writing down all your thoughts and confronting that passage over and over again, you will bring something into motion within you. At once, you will understand the Scripture passage in a different and deeper way.

I suggest two passages with which you can try this writing exercise: The first is the beginning of Psalm 23, "The LORD is my shepherd, I shall not want." This passage has a beautiful sound to it. But while you are writing it, perhaps you may stumble over it, "Is that really true, that I don't want for anything?" If you have this reaction, you can wrestle with the passage, change it around, and write it differently.

And then, quite consciously, you write the original passage. How does it sound now? Can you accept it? Does it express your reality? Does it change your attitude? If this passage is correct, how do you then deal with your loneliness, with your feeling of desolation, with your doubts, with the hurts of everyday life?

With these questions, you notice that this passage cannot simply be said or written thoughtlessly. It stirs something in you to movement. You must come to terms with it. And if you do that, it changes your attitude. It then creates your life anew.

The second passage is the beginning of Psalm 63: "O God, you are my God, I seek you, / my soul thirsts for you; / my flesh faints for you, / as in a dry and weary land where there is no water." If you write this passage down over and over, you come into contact with your yearning. On the one hand, you sense that this passage is too big for you. You absolutely cannot say it yet with full conviction.

On the other hand, however, this passage leads you down into the depth of your soul. There you discover within yourself a deep yearning for God. Your heart often longs for superficial things: for success, recognition, and love. But in the end, your soul longs for God.

If you write this passage over and over, you will become completely calm. And you will sense, "Yes, my soul thirsts for God." Without God your soul is like a land without water.

WEDNESDAY

CONTEMPLATE A FLOWER

FOR YOUR WEDNESDAY RITUAL, CONTEMPLATE A FLOWER. Wednesday corresponds to the third day of Creation, on which God made the land burst forth with new greenery and all sorts of plants and trees.

Choose a beautiful flower to contemplate. What do you see? You see beauty.

The Greek philosopher Plato says that in beauty one ultimately will see God's beauty. Of his very essence, God is beauty, truth, and goodness. All existence is ultimately true, beautiful, and good.

In the beauty of the flower, therefore, you discover something of God. God has created the flower. God's Spirit permeates the flower and makes it bloom. And the beauty that radiates out to you is the beauty of God. When you contemplate the flower, God's essence is revealed to you.

In the Christian tradition, flowers have also functioned as symbols, often for the saints. It is especially popular to associate flowers with Mary, the mother of God. Mary is compared to the rose, the lily, the daffodil, the daisy, the columbine, and the violet. All flowers have something to say about who Mary really is. The lily stands for purity and chastity, the violet for humility, the white rose for Mary as pure maid, the red rose for her love. The iris stands for her sorrows.

The columbine is also beloved in depictions of Mary. It was revered as a medicinal herb of the Germanic mother goddess, Freya. It indicates the healing that radiates from Mary. The lily of the valley, which frequently appears in pictures of Mary, is similarly a medicinal plant: it proclaims that Mary has borne the Savior of the world. The red carnation stands for the true and pure love that Mary embodies.

In the Litany of Loreto, Mary is referred to as *Rosa Mystica*, "Mystical Rose." And during the Middle Ages, people depicted Mary in the rose bower. In the West, the rose has a meaning similar to that of the lotus flower in Asia. In Greece, it is the flower of Aphrodite, the goddess of love. The rose, which enchants people with its scent, is thus a symbol for the love that fills us with wonderful fragrance. In ancient times, people wore wreaths of roses on their heads, not only for beauty's sake but also for medicinal purposes, because it was believed that the rose had cooling and mentally fortifying effects.

The late-medieval mystic Gertrude of Helfta calls Mary the "Rose of Love," and the "radiant rose of heavenly grace nourishes our souls with heavenly power." For the mystics, Mary as rose was a favorite image of union with God: "Rose completely immersed in God, you are inebriated on the drink of immense bliss." Thus wrote an anonymous fifteenth-century poet on the Lower Rhine. The image of the rose garden, so beloved by artists at that time, expresses the idea that Mary is full of love and that she radiates love.

Whether Mary sits under roses or she, herself, blooms as a rose, she drives out the winter of spiritual coldness from within us and makes our life blossom anew as in the spring. In the twelfth century, a pious poet put it this way: "When this beautiful rose, Mary, began to blossom, the winter of our sorrow came to an end and the summer of eternal joys and the May of everlasting delights began to appear, and with her the luscious green of paradise was given to us again."

And so in the image of the rose, the renewal of the cosmos merges with the bliss and happiness of humankind. Dante Alighieri was also filled with this vision when he called Mary the rose in which the eternal Word became flesh: "Within your womb was lit once more the flame of that love through whose warmth this flower opened to its full bloom in everlasting peace." For Dante, the Mystical Rose is symbol for the fusion of God's love with human love.

When I contemplate a flower, when I meditate on a rose, I am not conscious of all these wonderful thoughts of the mystics and poets. But I can simply allow to float to the surface the associations, images, and memories that are waiting to rise up in my soul. And so perhaps I recall the unique rose of which the Little Prince speaks and that he never forgets, because for him it is matchless. Or I may recall the song about Mary in which she wanders through a wood of thorns in order to transform it into a rose garden: "Then the thorns bore roses."

Meditating isn't thinking but imagining something that awakens in you all the images that lie ready in your soul—beautiful, healing images that put you more and more in touch with the unique, amazing image that God has made you for himself.

THURSDAY

BREAK BREAD

THE RITUAL OF BREAKING BREAD IS APPROPRIATE FOR Thursday. On Thursday, we remember the institution of the Lord's Supper, the Eucharist, when Jesus took bread, blessed it, broke it, and gave it to his disciples with the words, "This is my body that is for you. Do this in remembrance of me" (1 Cor 11:24).

When you break bread for yourself, you realize what happened at the Last Supper. And the Last Supper gives new meaning to your breaking of the bread.

Breaking bread is not only something practical, something we do in order to make it easier to eat the bread. Much more importantly, it is full of symbolism. I break the bread so that it will nourish me, so that I can live on it. I break apart something that is whole so that what is broken in me becomes whole.

Twenty years ago, at the dedication of our retreat house in Münsterschwarzach, the spiritual writer and theologian Henri Nouwen gave an impressive speech that touched us deeply. In his speech he meditated on four words: *take, bless, break, give*.

Jesus *took* the bread. We have all taken love. We have accepted God's love. And we have accepted love from our parents. Perhaps that love wasn't sufficient for us. But every person has accepted love from their parents, even if it was only the nine months spent in our mother's belly. It was love that led to our coming into existence, and that our mother summoned up for us when she carried us in her body. We are accepted by our parents and friends, we have accepted ourselves, and we know ourselves as accepted by God.

Jesus *blessed* the bread. All of us, too, are "blessed." To bless means to say good words. When we were baptized, God said these good words about us: "You are my beloved son. You are my beloved daughter. In you I am well pleased" (cf. Matt 3:17).

When I break bread in Thursday's ritual, I first take it carefully in my hands and bless it, like Jesus did. Then I get a sense of what "blessing" means. Blessing means that this bread nourishes me and strengthens me. God's blessing touches and fills me in the gifts of creation. God's blessing permeates me.

Each thing that I take to myself is blessed by God. By blessing the bread before I break it, I get a new feel for everything I eat. I take God's blessing in everything into myself.

Jesus *broke* the bread. In breaking the bread, I think of how I myself am broken. I experience myself as fragile. My body is fragile; it does not guarantee me health forever. My life history reveals breaks. Here a relationship is broken; there an ideal is broken: a life's dream in which I imagined how my life should be.

Henry Nouwen believes that in those places in which we are broken, all the armor with which we have surrounded our hearts—in order to protect ourselves from pain—shatters. There the masks that we wear and the roles that we play are shattered, and we are broken open in this way for the sake of our true self.

When the exterior shatters, the way to our interior is freed up. We are broken open for our brothers and sisters, we open ourselves for others, and we are broken open for God. Our images of God shatter, and we open ourselves for the incomprehensible God, who in all his incomprehensibility is, nevertheless, love—indeed, an incomprehensible love.

Jesus *gave* the bread to his disciples. Our love requires giving. Giving is an expression of fruitfulness.

Giving stands at the end; at the beginning stands taking. We can give only because we have taken. Taking and giving must exist in a balanced relationship to each other. The one who only takes swallows the wrong way or suffocates. The one who only gives over-exerts oneself.

I can give only because I am blessed and because I have received blessings. And even my brokenness is a condition for giving. One who is always successful, who has never experienced being broken and shattered, is in danger of orbiting only around oneself. Such a person has no need to give. Brokenness makes us capable of giving.

FRIDAY

GO THE WAY OF THE CROSS

LIVING MEANS BEING ON THE WAY; IT MEANS TO GO. Here on earth, we are only pilgrims and strangers. Abraham, the Father of our Faith, answered God's summons and set out on a journey. And his journey began with leaving behind what was familiar and trusted. The early monks understood this process as leaving behind all forms of dependency. Israel left Egypt, the land of their captivity, behind.

Furthermore, *to go* means to be always on the road, going in order to change. We cannot stand still or else we also stand still inwardly and become paralyzed. To go means to be on the way toward a goal: "Where are we going? Always home," said the poet, Novalis. In the end, we are always heading toward a goal beyond this world.

The road that we imagine and plan to travel is crossed again and again by the unforeseeable: by illness and by other interruptions in our life. Our life, too, is always at a crossroads—a way of the cross. The plans we imagine are thwarted, and what matters to us is to accept, in the cross, precisely the contrasts that are within us.

Jesus says, "If any want to become my followers, let them deny themselves and take up their cross and follow me" (Matt 16:24). Jesus understands our life as a journey. We are meant to follow Jesus on his journey.

In this regard, however, two attitudes are important. On the one hand, it is a matter of *becoming free of being ruled by one's own ego*. To go means to free oneself of the tyranny of one's own ego, which wants to rule over and decide everything.

On the other hand, it is a matter of *taking up our cross*. We must acknowledge the existence of the contrasts within us. We must let go of the illusion that we are only spiritual, only loving, only in control of ourselves and free. We are, at the same time, godless, empty, aggressive, out of control, and inwardly captive. This journey succeeds only if we make it as a way of the cross. We are invited to this through our Friday observance of the memory of Jesus's way of the cross and his death on the cross.

In monasteries with cloisters, monks have given concrete form to the mystery of Jesus's way of the cross. The monks walk slowly through the cloister in order to follow the mystery of the cross and the mystery of their journey. The way of the cross reminds the monks that they should allow themselves more and more to be broken open by the cross to the indescribable mystery of God.

According to the Gospel of John, the cross is a sign of the love that Jesus had for us to the end. By walking silently through the cloister, the monk yields to this love that touches everything in him: his heights and his depths, his light side and his shadow side, the depths of his soul and his daily conflicts. The cloister invites the monk to open himself, in his wandering, to the mystery of his redemption.

Reality happens in the midst of the confines and isolation of the monastery. There, in the cloister, the monk in his wandering meditates on the mystery of God's love. This love pervades everything earthly; it transforms everything in him and, time and again, it opens up heaven above the ordinariness and banality of his life. Thus, in the midst of his confined space, the monk can see the wideness of God; in his earthly journey, he can see heaven; and in the seclusion of the monastery, he can experience the eternal and indescribable Creator of the world.

There are five aspects on which you can meditate during this mindful walking:

1. With each step, imagine that you are journeying away from everything that holds you captive: from habits and relationships that do you no good, from the expectations of other people.
2. Keep going, slowly. You cannot stand still. In moving, you acknowledge that you are always on a journey. You cannot rest on your achievements.
3. Go your way just as you have imagined it. But be aware that your way does not always run so smoothly; many things can thwart it. Whatever thwarts your way will break you open more and more to God.
4. Go slowly and, while walking, do not lose your inner center—that place of stillness within. When we were

in the novitiate, our novice master counseled us to walk through the cloister after choral prayer as if we were carrying with us a precious bowl filled with the water of mercy. If you take this image with you when you go, your walk becomes something holy. You are carrying God with you into the world. You are then at the same time a monstrance that carries Christ himself into the world in a holy procession.

5. Imagine that you are always going toward God. While you go, meditate on the words of St. Paul: "But our citizenship is in heaven" (Phil 3:20).

6. Walking is a simple ritual. Do that which you do every day, but consciously. Go, choose specific routes, wander. Then you will experience that, through this slow and careful going, you are wandering more and more into the mystery of your redemption through Jesus Christ. It took place for us on the cross and will again and again happen anew.

SATURDAY

LISTEN TO MUSIC

IN THE JEWISH TRADITION, SATURDAY IS THE DAY OF Sabbath rest. Thus, human beings participate in God's Sabbath rest. The Christian tradition has transferred the theology of the Sabbath to Sunday; but it has also transferred part of the Jewish understanding of the Sabbath to Saturday. Saturday is dedicated to Mary's memory. Mary, the mother of God, denotes resting in God.

Christian tradition has always regarded Mary as the reverse of manly asceticism and work. Christians saw Mary, the mother who holds the Child in her arms. Mary was also always the contemplative woman. She is often depicted as reading. She ponders the mystery of God and humanity. There are pictures that portray Mary reading a book—presumably the Bible—while sitting on a donkey during the flight to Egypt. On Saturday, then, Mary invites us to contemplation.

Contemplation has many aspects. Since Marian devotion is always an optimistic spirituality, contemplation, too, which is associated with Mary, has something playful, exhilarating, free, and joyful about it. And so on Saturday, I invite you to listen totally consciously to music. Today, make a point of allowing some time to listen to music in all stillness.

Look for an appropriate piece of music. Whether you prefer the music of Johann Sebastian Bach, Wolfgang Amadeus Mozart, Ludwig van Beethoven, Georg Frideric Handel, Felix Mendelssohn, or Jean Sibelius, decide on the music your heart suggests to you. Then close your eyes and listen to the music. Let the music penetrate not only your ears but also your heart, indeed your entire body. Imagine the music permeating your entire body and making it swing and sing. Then you have an idea of what the Prophet Isaiah meant when he said, "Listen, so that you may live" (Isa 55:3). Music will drive away all your anxiety and despair, all your darkness and sadness.

Certainly, there is also music that is full of melancholy. Mozart composed melancholic melodies again and again. But by making the melancholy audible, he also transformed it—he did not remain trapped in it.

The music that permeates your body leads you to a new experience of yourself. Often, indeed, you feel that your body is full of tension and confused thoughts. But when your entire body is filled with music, it begins to vibrate. The Church fathers say that the rhythm of music puts rhythm into the soul. It leads the soul into the rhythm that corresponds to its nature.

All of life, too, is rhythm. Often enough we are thrown out of our rhythm. We feel burned out. Music lets the body settle once again into its own rhythm. This brings not only the body but also the soul to life.

Music gives wings to the soul. The Church father John Chrysostom expressed this wonderfully: "There is nothing like the melody of a song to lift up the soul, to give it wings, to free it from what is earthly, to release it from bodily captivity, to imbue it with love of wisdom, and to make it ignore and scorn everything that belongs to earthly existence." As St. Augustine noted, music ensures that "the people do not languish from a surfeit of grief." John Chrysostom is convinced that "the soul bears difficulties and troubles more easily when it sings or listens to a melody."

If you consciously listen to the second movement of Mozart's *Clarinet Concerto in A Major*, you will sense what it is like to overcome death. That for which we hope on Saturday—the resurrection of the dead—is audible in Mozart's music.

But in many arias from J.S. Bach's cantatas, this victory over death can also be heard. When I listen to these arias, I must not believe in the words as sung but, rather, allow the words as set to music fall into my heart. Then faith happens. What the words express becomes reality in my heart. At this moment, I don't need to reach a conclusion about faith. In the music there is simply *faith*. In listening to the music, faith becomes reality.

Let the music lift you out of your day-to-day problems. Then you sense that you are already now participating in God's Sabbath. Listen as Mary does, Mary who is our model for listening and believing. She listened to the sound of the angel's voice in such a way that the Word became flesh in her. In the same way, the music wants to "take flesh" in our body, so to speak. It wants to permeate and transform our thoughts and our actions, our speech and our feelings.

SUNDAY

EXPERIENCE STILLNESS

"GOD SAW EVERYTHING THAT HE HAD MADE, AND indeed, it was very good....And on the seventh day God finished the work that he had done, and he rested on the seventh day....So God blessed the seventh day and hallowed it" (Gen 1:31—2:3). Thus we read in the Creation story at the beginning of the Bible about the seventh day of the creation of the world. On Sunday, we take part in God's Sabbath rest.

But our Sundays are often hectic. We cram them with activities because we can't tolerate stillness. The Book of Genesis names three conditions in which stillness can succeed. The first condition: *God saw that everything was good.* Only when I affirm that my life is good—when I can also see the detours and wrong turns that ultimately were and are good for me—am I capable of becoming still. As long as I hear my inner voice of self-condemnation and self-rejection,

I will never get any peace. Then I am compelled to run even from stillness, because it becomes too threatening and unpleasant for me.

The second condition: *God blessed the seventh day.* The time of stillness is a blessed time. I place myself in the stillness under God's blessing. I imagine that God's blessing and God's love embrace me. Blessing is protection. In the stillness, I feel that God is watching over me. And blessing is fruitfulness. The time of stillness makes me fruitful. To bless means to say good words. In the stillness, I hear God's good word to me: "You are my beloved Son. You are my beloved daughter; with you I am well pleased" (cf. Mark 1:11).

The third condition: *God made the Sabbath holy.* The time of stillness is a holy time. Something holy is something that is withdrawn from the world. In stillness, the world—with its noise—has no access. There I am alone before God. For the ancient Greeks, only the holy was capable of healing. It is healthful for me to listen to the stillness.

The spiritual tradition distinguishes between silence and stillness, between *tacere* and *silentium*. Silence is a spiritual task. I hold my tongue. I decline to speak. I practice being silent. Stillness, on the other hand, is something preexisting. I enter into the stillness of a church, into the stillness of a forest, or into the stillness of the desert. My room in which I meditate breathes stillness. But I do not perceive the stillness if I am occupied with a thousand things. To that extent, silence and stillness belong together. I must be silent so that I can perceive the stillness.

But the still places do not only exist outside me; there is also a place of stillness in myself. The mystics tell us about this place. For the Desert Father Evagrius Ponticus, it is the place of God, the intuition of peace, a place filled with God's splendor and God's peace. For Johannes Tauler, it is the ground of one's soul; for Catherine of Siena, the inner cell; for Teresa of Avila, the innermost room of the interior castle. This place is within us, even if we do not feel it.

Make it your Sunday ritual to listen to the stillness. Sit in your room, in your prayer corner, or find a quiet place such as a church or a place away out in nature.

Then listen to the stillness that surrounds you. Sometimes there is an absolute silence in which you hear absolutely nothing. That is always a mysterious silence. But precisely when you sit in the woods or by a brook, you hear the murmur of the woods or the rushing of the brook. These sounds do not take away the stillness; they make it audible.

Enjoy the stillness that surrounds you. But then listen also to the stillness within you. As you slowly exhale, imagine that you are going through all the areas of your body and your soul, right to the ground of your soul. There is pure stillness.

You attain this stillness only when you pass through the noisy places in your heart. And you attain stillness only when you pass through your anger, through your anxiety, through your jealousy, through your guilt, and through your sadness. All the inner chaos may be there. You must not deny it. But don't get stuck there; go deeper, all the way to the ground of your soul, for there is where you find pure stillness.

Perhaps you sense this pure stillness only for a brief moment. Then the thoughts and feelings that occupy you return. But this brief moment of pure stillness—no thoughts about the stillness, just the stillness itself—frees you from the power of the world.

For Christians, this pure stillness is no empty stillness but a stillness that is filled with God and completed by the love and mercy of Jesus Christ. This love is more than a feeling. It is not necessary always to experience feelings when you perceive this pure stillness. You simply sense pure being. And this being is—as the philosophers and theologians tell us—always good, true, and beautiful. For Christians, this being is love at its deepest. In the cross, Christ's love has penetrated into the depths of this world—as well as into the depths of our soul—and now forms the true ground of everything that exists. This is how Jesus himself expresses it: "The kingdom of God is [already] among you" (Luke 17:21). Where the kingdom of God is in us, there God reigns over us and leads us to our true self. He frees us from the power of the world.

When you perceive this stillness, then you experience your self anew. There are five ways you can do this:

1. *You are free.* Free from the power of other people, from their expectations and demands, from their estimations and opinions of you. You stop thinking about what others think of you. You are simply there, without the pressure of having to justify yourself.
2. *You are healed and whole.* In this place of stillness, no one can hurt you. People's hurtful words don't reach here. And even the wounds caused by your life history cannot touch this holy place.
3. *You are original and authentic.* All the images that others have projected onto you, all the images with which they have darkened your existence, dissolve. But even your images of self-devaluation, in which

you make yourself small, and the images in which you overestimate yourself, raise yourself above your own existence and ultimately make excessive demands on yourself, dissolve. You are allowed simply to be. You do not need to prove yourself to anyone. You are simply yourself, just as God has made you. You are in touch with the original, genuine, intact image of God in you.

4. *You are pure and clear.* No guilty feelings can penetrate this place of stillness; and even the guilt that you may have laid upon yourself cannot disturb this space.

5. *You feel at home.* Because this space of stillness is where God lives, God is always inexpressible Mystery. And only where this Mystery is, are you at home.

SEVEN RITUALS
for the
SECOND WEEK

MONDAY

MEDITATE ON YOUR OWN BIRTH

THE WORK WEEK BEGINS ON MONDAY. FOR MANY people, Monday is a dreary day. It's the day after the weekend, when the daily routine begins all over, and once again one finds oneself in the treadmill of ordinary life.

A good ritual for this day of beginnings is to meditate on your own birth; so close your eyes and imagine that you have just been born. Imagine yourself coming forth from your mother's womb. The baby sees sunlight for the first time. He greets the world with a cry. His mother presses him to her breast to comfort him, and she looks at this newborn child.

In this child, a unique human being is born. In this child, a unique individual is born. She has not yet been determined and formed by her upbringing. Everything in her is new. The seeds of new possibilities are planted in her. She is not predetermined to a particular fate. Everything is possible for this child. Everything is new, untouched, and genuine.

This original, perfect child is within you. Try to make contact with this child. Imagine that you are beginning this week with this inner child. You are not determined by the roles that you play in your family, at your place of work, or in your circle of friends. You are not determined by what you have done up until now, by your upbringing, or by the events that have left their stamp on your life.

Naturally, you have been molded by your history. You have developed certain characteristics. But within you is also this newborn child. Within you is the potential to be completely new and completely authentic.

Imagine the little child in his mother's arms. He is under no pressure to be or to do a particular thing. He does not have to prove himself. He is simply the way he is.

If you get in touch with this child within you, you become free from the pressure of proving yourself to others. You don't bend a certain way when you enter your workplace. You do not consider what the others expect of you or how you should behave so that the others will be satisfied with you. You are simple. You are free. You go into this day and live what is within you. You are in touch with your intact, genuine, original, and perfect inner child.

Today you will do what you do every Monday. You know what awaits you at work. But when you are in contact with your inner child, everything becomes different. Everything takes on the flavor of the new and authentic. You simply do what you do—without ulterior motives, without considering what the others may say about it.

The newborn child in you is curious. She investigates everything; she sees and grasps everything because everything is new and strange. With this image in your mind, take the matters of this day in hand and shape them simply according to their nature. Then your work will become new and creative, and in it you will imitate the creative work of God, who makes all things new.

TUESDAY

Think about Your Guardian Angel

IN EARLIER TIMES, THE CHURCH DEVOTED TUESDAY TO the angels. And so a good ritual for today is to meditate on your personal guardian angel.

"Take care that you do not despise one of these little ones; for, I tell you, in heaven their angels continually see the face of my Father in heaven" (Matt 18:10). In their commentaries on these words of Jesus, the Church fathers tell us that when we were born, God placed an angel at our side. This angel accompanies us on our earthly journey. He watches over and protects us and, when we die, carries us over the threshold of death into God's arms.

Angels are spiritual, created beings and personal forces. They are not persons who can be stood side by side and counted. They are messengers that God sends us so that we may feel his healing presence. The angel that God has placed at our side puts us in touch with all the abilities that God has placed in our soul. He is the companion of our soul who opens up to us our soul's potential.

Consider that your guardian angel accompanies you wherever you go. He is no guarantee that no physical harm will come to you, but he most certainly protects your inner core. He accompanies you on your life paths, even when you take detours or wrong turns from time to time. He puts up with you even when you can't put up with yourself. He is your inner companion.

Imagine your guardian angel going with you when you leave the house, when you ride in your car, or when you take a long trip. Ask your guardian angel to support you in a difficult situation.

In your meditation, you can either ask your guardian angel himself to give you the right words, or you can pray to God that, during this conversation, he will send you the words that will guide the conversation in a good direction. And you can keep in mind that you are not alone in this conversation, but that your angel is with you.

You don't see your angel. The angel comes from God. God sends him. But through your angel, God's healing presence accompanies you. Your angel is always a protective angel. He protects you from the sometimes distressing presence of unpleasant or hostile people. He protects you from their aggression, from their destructive tendencies, from their insulting words. Imagine that your angel is wrapping you, so to speak, in a protective mantle that deflects all the injurious impulses that come from the outer world and shields you from the cold that sometimes flows your way.

Your angel is God's messenger. Not for a single moment does God ever leave you alone. He sends you a messenger. This messenger can be an inner impulse, an inner certainty, or even the sense of being supported and protected. This messenger is your angel whom God has placed at your side. Your angel shows you that God is friendly to people, and is a God who accompanies you in all the situations of your life. If you start your day being conscious of this, you will proceed more attentively. You will listen more attentively to your soul. You will see each situation in a new light.

You are not alone, and the people you meet are not alone. They, too, have their guardian angel. They, too, are surrounded by God's love. At their side, God has also placed an angel. If you imagine this concretely, then your encounters will change and your meetings take on a new hue. On your journeys, you are not alone but watched over and protected by your guardian angel. This relieves you of all tension and frees you from being anxious that something unpleasant could happen to you. And at the same time, it makes you more mindful.

WEDNESDAY

ACT MINDFULLY

O N WEDNESDAY, THE CHURCH REMEMBERS ST. JOSEPH, the model worker. And so I invite you today to take a word of St. Benedict with you into your work. Benedict of Nursia establishes the following rule for the Cellarer, the person responsible for the monastery's finances: "Let him regards all the utensils of the monastery and its whole property as if they were the sacred vessels of the altar" (*Rule of Benedict* 31:10). This mindfulness is an important theme. Spiritual writers of all religions write today about mindfulness.

Today, practice this mindfulness at your work. When you pick up your pen to write, be aware of what you are doing. You are pick-ing up a tool that helps you to write. Then devote yourself entirely to your writing. When you write, words are produced. These should not simply be empty words, but words that give life. When you turn on your computer, handle it attentively. It makes your work easier. Even if it is a technical tool, it shows you something of the wisdom of God that has gone into its devising. When you use the programs on your computer, do so mindfully. Be thankful for the many possibilities that the computer offers you.

When the telephone rings, be mindful when you pick up the call. Do not do it absentmindedly. Stop your work. Give your attention to the person who is calling and with whom you are now speaking. Even though you don't see them, you hear their voice and they hear you. They sense if you are listening attentively and engaging with them or if you are impatiently trying to bring the conversation to an end.

When someone knocks on your door, be attentive to the person who enters. Be present to them. Close the "door" to the work that you have just been doing. Open your inner door to the person who has just entered so that you are completely in the moment and engaged with the person. This way the meeting will succeed. When you leave your office, be mindful of the steps you take. You are now freeing yourself from all demands and concerns. You are completely in the zone. And when you open the door to return to your office, do it mindfully. The door may also open your heart so that you can totally devote yourself to your work.

The ritual of mindfulness is one that you can practice throughout the day. Nevertheless, it helps when you start your morning with a mindfulness meditation. For this, calmly sit down and be mindful only of this moment and what is happening in it. You breathe in and breathe out. You are completely in the moment.

If you start your morning with this mindfulness ritual, you

will be able to continue it during the day as well. Everything that you touch—your pen, your computer, the hammer with which you hammer a nail, the scissors with which you cut something, the door, your briefcase, your books and papers—you touch mindfully and with care. You are in relationship with the things that you touch and with what you are doing. You will sense that this mindfulness does you good and that it gives your workday a new character.

Your relationship with God will flow into all your concrete actions, because in everything you touch, you ultimately sense an intimation of God. The Apostle Paul had this in mind when he told the Greek philosophers on the Areopagus to "search for God and perhaps grope for him and find him—though indeed he is not far from each one of us. For 'In him we live and move and have our being'; as even some of your own poets have said" (Acts 17:27–28). Human beings can find God in all things. If you live mindfully, you feel God in everything that is. In all creatures you touch the Creator. God is not far from us; he is in everything that exists.

THURSDAY

GIVE THANKS

ON THURSDAY, WE COMMEMORATE THE INSTITUTION of the Eucharist. *Eucharist* means "to give thanks." Therefore, I invite you to a ritual of thanksgiving.

Sit down and begin by giving thanks for your body. Breathe and pay attention to your breathing. Sense the life within you. Allow your breath to permeate your body. Rest in yourself.

Now give thanks for the health that God has given you. And if you are in pain, thank God that the pain reminds you of your true self, your inner core that is not touched by pain. The pain also reminds you of God, who supports you in your pain.

Go through the story of your life. Give thanks for your childhood, even if everything wasn't ideal. You have lived through something that only you have lived through. You have experienced something that only you have experienced. Thus, you have become an experienced person, one who knows the mystery of being human. Give thanks for your parents and for all that you received and learned through them. Give thanks for your life's journey.

Thank God that he has never in your life left you alone, even if you have sometimes felt alone. Thank God for his guidance. Now, in hindsight, you will recognize God's guidance that you did not sense while going through the many dark valleys of your life. Give thanks for the people that God has sent you: for your parents and grandparents, for your spouse, for your children, for your friends, for the people whom you have encountered and in whom you have recognized something of the mystery of humanity, for all the people who have inspired and given to you.

Finally, get up and stand in front of the mirror. Look yourself in the face, without making a value judgment about whether you are attractive enough. Look at your face and thank God for your uniqueness. Your face is one of a kind. There is no other face that looks exactly like yours.

Look right through your face to the ground of your soul. Who is there, looking you in the face? Who is this unique, one-of-a-kind person? Where is this authentic image of God in you? Then give thanks for your face; thank God that you are this unique person. Thank God for the depth that meets you in your face, for the beauty that radiates toward you, for the experiences of joy and sorrow, of love and disappointment that have formed this face and that are imprinted on it.

Next, hold up your hands and look at them. Not only in your face, but also in these hands of yours, your life has left its mark. All your experiences are accumulated in them. In our hands, we are able to see our own truth. Your hands have a life line, a health line, and a relationship line.

Regard your hands and consider all that these hands have already formed and shaped: what they have grasped, and, along the way, what they have brought, created, and performed. Thank God for your hands and for everything that you have accomplished with these hands. And thank God for everything that he has placed into your hands: for the power, for the dexterity, for the tenderness that they can express, and for the security that they give. Your hands can point, write, grasp, feel, caress, receive, give....Look at the miracle of your hands and thank God for everything that these hands have received and given.

FRIDAY

EMBRACE THE WORLD

ON FRIDAY, WE ARE MINDFUL OF JESUS'S DEATH ON the cross. The cross reminds many people of sorrow and burdens; but the early Church fathers regarded it as a sign of hope, salvation, and consummated love. The Gospel of John presents Jesus's death on the cross as an expression of the love he had for us right to the end.

The cross is an image of Jesus's devotion to the human race. At the same time, it symbolizes how Jesus on the cross embraces all the contrasts in this world, that he embraces and accepts the contrasts in us with his love, and that he embraces and unites the entire cosmos. The Church fathers speak of the "outstretched" Logos, who unites the world's contrasts. An ancient second-century text praises the cross with these words: "O name of the cross, you who encompass the universe within yourself! Hail to you, O cross, for holding the total extent of the cosmos together."

I propose two rituals with which you can meditate on the mystery of the cross. *In the first ritual,* you look at the cross in your home. Perhaps you also have a picture with an expressive image of the cross. Reflect on how Jesus gave himself up to the cross for you. He also died for you out of love. In the Gospel of John, Jesus says, "No one has greater love than this, to lay down one's life for one's friends" (John 15:13).

When you reflect on this love that Jesus gave his friends, you sense how precious you are. Someone has risked his life for you because he loves you to the end. When you look at the cross, leave all self-reproaches and self-devaluation aside. You have inestimable value. You are so precious that Jesus died for you. His love is unconditional. He loves you just as you are, with your faults and weaknesses. So you have no need to reproach yourself for your faults. The cross shows you that everything in you is accepted.

This love, the Church fathers tell us, encompasses not only all the contrasts in the world but also the contrasts in ourselves. Everything in you is embraced by the love you see in Jesus.

The mystery of the passion that invites us to consider the cross of Jesus has seen that love first of all. Naturally, in Christ on the cross we also see the Man of Sorrows. But the spirituality of the passion has regarded this sorrow as an expression of the love that encompasses us. Jesus has suffered for us. Already the First Letter of St. Peter tells us, "Christ also suffered for you....For you were going astray like sheep, but now you have returned to the shepherd and guardian of your souls" (1 Pet 2:21–25). The sacrifice of Jesus on the cross is the place in which we find our home, in which we go home to him who shepherds our souls and cares for them. It is the place in which we return home to ourselves, to our soul, and to our true self.

In the second ritual, stand upright and stretch out your hands at shoulder height, so that the palms of your hands are facing forward. This is the gesture in which Jesus is pictured on the cross. For the Church fathers, this image showed Jesus embracing and encompassing the entire world with his outstretched arms.

When you stand in this position, you can imagine that you, too, are embracing the entire world. Everything in the cosmos, in nature, and in the universe is also in you. There is a saying in Latin, *Nihil humanum mihi alienum*, which means, "Nothing human is foreign to me." In this gesture you can say to yourself, "Nothing cosmic is foreign to me." You embrace the entire world. This gives you wideness and freedom. You need not reject anything. Everything in you is embraced by Christ's love—and the entire world is full of Christ's love.

Both in yourself and in the cosmos, you touch the love of Jesus who, from the cross, flows into everything that exists. Thus, you no longer need to battle against anything within yourself—neither against your anxiety, nor against your sexuality. With Christ's love, you embrace everything that is in you. Thus, everything is transformed and healed. Everything is allowed to be.

Perhaps you find this arms-outstretched position to be taxing. It becomes easier if you center yourself, so to speak, and spread your arms out wide from your center, just as a tree spreads its branches from its trunk. In this gesture, you are embracing the entire world as well as all the contrasts within you. You are also embracing the entire human race. You exclude no one from your love because Christ on the cross excluded no one from his love. On the cross, he embraced everyone.

SATURDAY

Bury the Old

ON SATURDAY, WE RECALL HOLY SATURDAY, THE DAY on which Christ lay in the grave. A dream about a grave is an invitation to bury something old. And so today I invite you to a burial ritual. Consider what you would like to bury: which conflict, which prejudices, which reproaches against others? Then make a list of everything you would like to bury. Simply write without thinking of putting things in any order.

You will see that many things that you would like to bury will surface. All the insults come out. When you think of these insults, you are completely in the past. You feel insulted or you sense that much is unfinished. There is much that I haven't reappraised from the past: being misunderstood in my family or my circle of friends, unjust treatment at work, the breakdown of a relationship, abandonment, sorrow over the death of a dear person, and so on.

Take twenty minutes to write down everything that surfaces in your heart and that you carry around with you and that is still unfinished. Then read through your list one more time. Find a place in your garden or somewhere nearby. With a small spade, dig a hole and bury the crumpled piece of paper. If you wish, you can also plant something here that reminds you of what you have buried. The things you have buried become fertilizer for something new that wants to blossom in you.

You can also take the paper on which you have written this list and burn it, and then bury the ashes or use them to fertilize a tree, a bush, or a flower. Then stay a while at that spot and tell yourself, "Yes, I have buried everything. I don't want to dig it up anymore. I'm leaving it there. Even if it comes to mind again, I won't trouble myself about it anymore. I have buried it and I'm leaving it buried. I believe that Christ takes me by the hand and raises me up so that I take part in his resurrection."

Another kind of burial ritual is a gesture in which you hold your hands out in front of you in the form of a bowl. In doing so, look at your hands and see the wounds of life by which someone may have fixed you into a particular image or category, and you feel trapped. Your hand wounds may also result from situations in which someone hit you, as well as from times when someone took away a protective and helping hand and let you fall.

Then turn your hands around so that your palms are facing downward. Assuming this position, imagine letting go of what burdens you; letting go of what has hurt you in the past. You refuse to use these things to reproach others or as an excuse not to live your life. In this gesture, also let go of the life patterns that hinder you from living fully: your perfectionism, your tendency always to blame yourself. Let go of reproaching yourself, blaming yourself, and tormenting yourself. Bury everything that hinders your life. Bury it in the grave of Jesus Christ, so that he, through his resurrection, will transform it and allow you to rise up as a new human being.

SUNDAY

MEDITATE ON THE SUN

ON SUNDAY, WE RECALL THE RESURRECTION OF JESUS. The Church fathers have compared Jesus's resurrection to the rising sun. For them, the sun that rises every morning is a symbol of the resurrection, in which Jesus illuminates all the darkness in the world and in us with his light.

The Letter to the Ephesians quotes an early Christian baptismal hymn in which the risen Christ is compared with the light that shines on us: "Sleeper, awake! Rise from the dead, and Christ will shine on you" (Eph 5:14). In baptism, we participate in Jesus's resurrection. "For once you were darkness, but now in the Lord you are light. Live as children of light" (Eph 5:8). This passage refers to us.

While the Romans called the first day of the week *dies dominica* (the Lord's day), the Germanic Christians named the first day of the week "Sunday" (the sun's day). For them, the sun was the image through which they understood the resurrection.

Today, meditate on the sun. If the sun is shining, then stand or sit in its light. Let the sun warm you. Imagine that, through the sun, God's love is radiating toward you. It is God's love that warms your skin. You are standing in the sun. You are completely, totally surrounded by its light and warmth. Then imagine the sun going through your skin and warming your entire body. In that warmth, you feel God's love. Let this love flow into your whole body. Then you will feel that everything in you is permeated by God's love. There is nothing in you that God's love does not touch. This is the mystery of the resurrection.

The icons of the Eastern Church portray the resurrection as an event in which Jesus descends into the nether world, takes the dead by the hand, and leads them to the light. So you, too, can imagine that Jesus, in the light of the sun, lovingly touches everything in you and says, "This, too, may be. This, too, I have taken up in my death and my resurrection so that it comes to life."

The sun does not only symbolize the love that the resurrection mystery calls stronger than death; it also stands for the light. And so you can imagine that, in the light of the sun, Christ touches everything in you so that everything in you can come to the light. In the light of the sun, Christ descends into all the dark spaces in your body and your soul, in order to bring to the light and into life everything that is numb, suppressed, and repressed.

Perhaps you have the feeling that there are closed-off spaces in your body to which you yourself have no entry. These, then, are dark spaces in which lie things that are suppressed and repressed. Perhaps you yourself fear these places, because what is repressed can explode and cause everything to crumble. Imagine how the light of the sun shines into these dark regions of your body, in the dark rooms of your being, and illumines everything. The warm sunlight can bring order to the chaos and transform what is dangerous into an intimate friend. You lose your fears. Then there is nothing within you that is not illumined by the sun.

Jesus gives us a basis for why we can let go of all our fear of ourselves and of those who can discover what is repressed in us: "So have no fear of them; for nothing is covered up that will not be uncovered, and nothing secret that will not become known" (Matt 10:26). The light of the resurrection sun illuminates all the darkness, uncovers all that is hidden. So we need have no more fear, either of what is unknown in us or of those who can divulge what is hidden behind our attractive façade. In his resurrection, Christ himself opens the closed rooms of our body and our soul, in order to place everything in the light of God's love.

What we keep hidden behind closed doors is something missing from our true vitality. Many people live only a small part of the potential that is available to them. The risen Christ will bring everything in us to life. He has come so that we "may have life, and have it abundantly" (John 10:10).

When you allow the sun of the resurrection to shine totally through you, you get some idea of the mystery of the resurrection, of this life at its fullest, of the love that is stronger than death, and of the light of Jesus that illumines everything in us.

EVENING RITUAL

Embrace Everything

RITUALS CLOSE ONE DOOR AND OPEN ANOTHER. THE morning ritual opens the door that lets our day become blessed. The task of the evening ritual is to close the door of the day so that the door of the night can be opened.

For the early monks, the night was always something holy. They respected the stillness of the night, for in the night's stillness God might speak to them in dreams. And the night's quiet is the place in which God wants to touch our heart. And so a lovely evening ritual is to close the door of the day by crossing your hands over your chest. As noted below, this gesture has different meanings. When you make this gesture, you should not meditate on all of its meanings at once, but rather decide on one meaning.

Crossing the arms over the chest recalls the cross of Christ. The gesture of the cross is ultimately a gesture of embrace. In John's

Gospel, Jesus says, "And I, when I am lifted up from the earth, will draw all people to myself" (John 12:32). On the cross, Jesus embraces us. He embraces all the contrasts in us. He also embraces what is hurt, sick, and suffering in us.

The gesture of the cross is an expression of love with which Jesus on the cross loved us to the end. I take on Jesus's embrace on the cross by crossing my hands over my chest. I embrace myself because Christ on the cross has embraced me.

I would like to describe to you four ways of interpreting this embrace:

1. *Embracing contrasts.* Because Christ on the cross has embraced me with my contrasts, I embrace in myself everything that contrasts. I embrace what is strong and what is weak, the healthy and the sick, the whole and the broken, the successes and the failures, the lived and the unlived, the lively and the numb, the fulfilled and the unfulfilled, the confidence and the fear, the joy and the sorrow, the hope and the despair, the known and the unknown, the light and the dark. By embracing all the contrasts within me, I accept myself—along with all that is in me—and I say goodbye to the illusion of being only strong, only healthy, and only pious.

    Suppressing our contrasts and holding to our illusions make us sick. By accepting ourselves with our contrasts because we are accepted by Christ, we become whole and entire, healthy and free within. We no longer need to suppress. Everything within us is allowed to be, because everything in us is embraced by Christ's love on the cross.

2. *Embracing the wounded child.* We all have within us a little child. It often cries out when we are wounded. The abandoned child cries out when a "goodbye" is coming or when we are afraid that someone who is dear to us might abandon us. The child who is ignored appears when we are ignored by our boss or by our spouse.

But we are not only wounded children. We are also human beings with paternal and maternal instincts. And as fathers and mothers, we are responsible for the wounded child in us. We must take care of that child. In our evening gesture, we embrace our inner wounded child.

So imagine yourself embracing the abandoned child within, as well as the ridiculed child, the devalued child, the child who got a raw deal, the overworked child, the helpless child, the neglected child, the shamed child, the child who was beaten, the rejected child. And allow yourself to be led from the wounded child to the divine child within.

In each of us there also dwells the divine child. This child knows exactly what is good for us. He or she represents the original, authentic image of ourselves that God has placed within us. The divine child leads me into the inner space of stillness where I come into contact with the unique, inviolate, genuine image that God has made of me, and reveals to me the untarnished brilliance of God within me. The divine child leads me into that quiet space in which I realize that I am free, whole and complete, original and authentic, pure and clear, and at home.

By embracing my wounded child and letting myself be led to the divine child within, I become calm. The wounded child no longer cries out but finds peace in my protecting hands. And the divine child allows me to be thankful for my life, which, despite all the injuries I have sustained, is whole and complete, unique and valuable.

3. *Embracing the day just finished.* I embrace everything I experienced today, and I renounce any temptation to judge what has happened. I let Christ embrace everything and I embrace it myself as well. I embrace the encounters that have gifted or wounded me, my appropriate and inappropriate reactions, my successes and my setbacks, my peacefulness and restlessness, what I was able to accomplish and what I postponed, the good interactions and the conflicts. I embrace this day and give it over to God.

4. *Hiding in God's arms.* The gesture of embrace also reminds me that at night I let myself fall into God's good hands. I imagine that tonight I am in God's good hands. These hands carry me. In them I am secure, held, and loved. I do not need to prove anything. I can let myself go. I can let go of all my cares and fears in order to hide myself in God's loving hands.

But God's hands are also embracing hands. Just as I now embrace myself, so too will God embrace me in this night. God's hands will protect me and lovingly embrace me.

Regardless of which of the four interpretations you choose to meditate on, conclude this evening ritual with an ancient evening blessing that the Church used for nearly sixteen hundred years. Even today, this tender, ancient text manages to touch me. A blessing always communicates God's loving concern for us, so speak it slowly:

Lord,
enter this house and let your holy angel dwell here.
Guard us in peace, and may your holy blessing
always be upon us, and around us, and in us.
We ask this through Christ our Lord. Amen.